Educators' Guide

The Curious Kids and the Squiggly Question:

A Storybook Approach to Introducing Research Skills

Written By:

Marilyn P. Arnone

Sharon Coatney

With illustrations from the storybook by Gerry Stockley

LIBRARIES UNLIMITED
A Member of the Greenwood Publishing Group
Westport, Connecticut • London

ISBN 1-59158-197-4

LIBRARIES UNLIMITED
A Member of the Greenwood Publishing Group, Inc.
88 Post Road West
Westport, CT 06881
www.lu.com

TABLE OF CONTENTS

INTRODUCTION

Welcome

Acknowledgements

Book Summary

Goals

Using This Guide

Making the Most of the Storybook

INTRODUCTION

Welcome

We hope you find this guide has ideas that will stimulate your own creativity in exciting students as they begin digging for answers to their research questions.

Research often happens in conjunction with class assignments. But children can learn so much in informal settings, as well, especially if they use some of the skills they learn in school. Children choosing to investigate a topic on their own time and for the enjoyment of learning is the basis of *The Curious Kids and the Squiggly Question*. We know that children "wonder." It is this unique attribute of young children that we support with this new series of books. The Curious Kids books will support and encourage that wonder, furnishing the skills needed to find out the answers to all their "squiggly questions." Each book will introduce a significant part of the research process, helping kids learn how to learn. This storybook focuses on the *beginning stage* of research in which children define their research questions and formulate a research plan. It serves as a catalyst for an entire research project on caterpillars and butterflies or on insects. This guide picks up where the storybook leaves off providing teaching ideas that can be used throughout the entire research process (i.e., beginning, during, and *ending stage*s of research).

Acknowledgements

In addition to the acknowledgements made in the storybook, there are also several educators who contributed specifically to this educators' guide in the form of teaching ideas, lesson plans, and inspiration. We wish to thank Marie Sciretta, Michele Messenger, Jean Maier, and Karen Leo for their creativity and professionalism.

Book Summary

The curious kids have identified an information need. The have to learn about caterpillars so they can find out how to keep Squiggly alive. So, that's their big question. But to answer it, they will need to become information detectives using their research skills.

The characters in the book take listeners/readers through the *beginning stage* of research in which a topic or question is identified, the research focus is narrowed down to make it more manageable, and a plan is made for such things as

identifying a range of potential, relevant types of information sources to be explored. In the story, Chen wonders if there might be information he can use from his comic books. Tanisha explains why comic books would not be an appropriate source of info. Part of their planning process is thinking of ideas for how they might present or communicate their information once they have completed their research. The Curious Kids experience some of the common feelings associated with research. At first, they are excited about the topic they will investigate--caterpillars…and how to keep Squiggly (who they rescued from the playground) alive.

> **"In order to save Squiggly, we need INFORMATION! Are you ready to start an information adventure?" exclaims Timmy.**

Often, initial confidence can wane as students become confused with a topic so big they are unsure of where to start. For the Curious Kids consulting with Mac, Information Detective, seemed a logical stop on their journey. They knew he could help them. Mac suggested brainstorming and it helped. They defined the big question but Tanisha was frustrated:

> **"Caterpillars is a BIG Topic; there's so much to know about them. I still don't know where to start our research!" she blurted out.**

Mac has a tendency to get off track and the kids had all they could do to keep him focused. Once they learn to make a plan, things start hopping. As can be expected research can be frustrating at points. Where do you start? It seems there is so much to accomplish! The storybook sets up the *beginning stage* of research and motivates listeners to want to continue researching caterpillars and butterflies. If the story were to continue, Chen, Timmy, and Tanisha would enter the *during stage* of the research process -- exploring, collecting, and organizing information. It is at this point, that Carol Kulhthau (1991) has documented frustration in older children as they discover discrepancies between their existing knowledge and new information. It is important to include teaching strategies that will help bolster student confidence at this stage. As their uncertainty is resolved (about midway through the process) confidence re-emerges.

Goals

There are several broad goals for this and other storybooks and guides in this series: They are:

> To stimulate the natural curiosity (immediate) of young children and foster the disposition to continue to be curious (long-range). The type of curiosity

that, in order to be resolved or satisfied, requires the application of research and information literacy skills.

To introduce information literacy skills that will enable children to satisfy their curiosity and encourage a continuing motivation to inquire and learn.

To provide the above in the context of curriculum-related topics that can be explored both in and out of school.

To use a storybook approach to integrate information literacy with early literacy skills and curriculum related content.

As a result of listening to *The Curious Kids and the Squiggly Question* and engaging in activities (from the guide) to reinforce and expand their learning, children should demonstrate curiosity for learning more about caterpillars, butterflies and bugs. Specific information literacy objectives include:

Students can:

- Articulate the big topic or question
- State some of the smaller questions
- Identify several sources for finding information
- Know whether some sources can be trusted or not
- Display higher order thinking skills regarding applying skills in everyday life
- Decide whether a source is useful in answering their questions.
- Make a preliminary plan for their research
- Think about a way to share their research with others

Literacy objectives include the following:

Students can:

- Listen attentively to spoken language
- Listen attentively for a specified period of time
- Listen to gain information
- Listen critically to understand
- Speak in response to the reading of imaginative and informational texts
- Participate in group discussions

The teaching ideas and lesson plans in this guide integrate information literacy objectives with specific subject areas such as language arts and science. Using the Mid-continent Research for Education and Learning (McREL) national content standards, each teaching idea or lesson plan identifies one or more standards that it addresses.

Using This Guide

This guide is designed to help you incorporate the read-aloud experience of *The Curious Kids and the Squiggly Question* with teaching research and information literacy skills in the context of a curriculum unit on caterpillars and butterflies. It could also be integrated into an overall unit on insects.

As mentioned earlier, the storybook focuses on skills for the *beginning stage* of a research project. Thus, it is an excellent catalyst for getting started on a research project involving both the classroom teacher and library media specialist. This guide expands on the storybook and offers ideas and lesson plans for continuing the research through the "during" and "ending" stages. When necessary, the guide also indicates which activities are more appropriate for K-1 or 2-3. Here is what is coming up in this guide:

> <u>Part I</u> offers teaching ideas and lesson plans for the *beginning stage* of research including what's my big question, what are my little questions, and what's my plan. It begins with several activities that address comprehension of the storybook. It also includes teaching some basic information that students need to know into order to plan the most appropriate search strategies and select resources. For example, one teaching idea describes an activity for teaching students to distinguish fiction from nonfiction in a way that gains and sustains their motivation even after the lesson is completed.
>
> <u>Part II</u> focuses on ideas and lesson plans that would be appropriate in the *during stage* of research when children are exploring and digging for answers to their smaller questions. Teaching ideas for helping young children to locate sources, extract ideas, collect and evaluate information, observe and take notes, etc. For example, you will find a lesson on introducing the Dewey Decimal System in a fun way and teaching ideas that involve hands-on experiences in data collection.
>
> <u>Part III</u> focuses on the *ending stage* of research. It offers ideas for ways in which students ranging from kindergarten through third grade could present their research. Examples include the creation of a caterpillar/butterfly picture dictionary as a class, a story web, riddles and a class Web page on caterpillars and butterflies positioning students as the experts on the subject and incorporating many of their discoveries.

Making the Most of the Storybook

Here is a recipe for enhancing the learning experiences that come from both reading the story for early literacy competencies (e.g. listening for information and understanding) and being introduced to a critical information literacy skill. Look for this recipe as a help found in each of the books in the Mac, Information Detective series, starting with *The Strangest Dinosaur That Never Was*.

RECIPE

ENHANCING THE LEARNING EXPERIENCE OF READING

THE CURIOUS KIDS AND THE SQUIGGLY QUESTION

1. PLAN (you)
2. PREPARE (students)
3. READ (the story)
4. REINFORCE (learning)

Planning Ahead

- Prepare yourself by reading the story before introducing it to students, taking note of the vocabulary list and the placement within the story of the *Interactive Pages.*
- Decide ahead of time how you will use the *Interactive Pages,* considering the age of your students and time constraints. There are two ways of utilizing them. Of course, you may choose to adapt or combine the two to satisfy your particular situation.

    1. Use them as reflection points. Get children to brainstorm ideas and participate. Brainstorming helps to increase relevance.

    2. Use them as pausing points. While the *Interactive Pages* are excellent places to get children to interact and process the events of the story by using retelling and discussion, they are also natural pausing places which can be used as a place to pick up the story when you have the next opportunity with your students. If you decide to use an *Interactive*

Page as a pausing place, make sure you leave students thinking about the question posed on the *Interactive Page* as they will create a "cliffhanger" of sorts to pique continued student interest. Pausing places may also be useful for the very youngest children with shorter attention spans.

Note your thoughts on using the Interactive Pages:

___

___

___

___

- Prepare a comfortable read aloud environment in which students feel at ease with asking questions, brainstorming etc. Sometimes this can be accomplished with seating, by creating a special storytelling corner, by the types of posters you have lining the walls, and by displaying interesting artifacts to interest students in the story being considered. Using a rug, individual carpet squares or a low bookcase can also help define a special area.

Note your ideas for creating a comfortable storytelling environment:

___

___

___

___

___

- Create positive anticipation for reading the story. One way is to display a poster/coloring sheet of Squiggly or the book cover of *The Curious Kids and the Squiggly Question* in your LMC or classroom. There are many ideas. Use your own creativity…

Note your ideas for creating positive anticipation for reading *The Curious Kids and The Squiggly Question:*

___

___

___

___

Preparing Students For The Story

Hopefully, by now some of your students have started asking questions about your squiggly caterpillar poster. So, you have stimulated their curiosity. This can occur a day or so beforehand or even on the very day you intend to read them the story. Before reading the story, there are a few things you can do to prepare students and increase the learning potential of this read aloud experience.

1. Set the stage for the story. Tell the students that an important part of learning to read is thinking about and predicting what a story will be about.

> **PREDICTION ACTIVITY**
>
> Using only the storybook, a marker and large chart paper, have students make predictions about the story based only on the book cover. Introduce evidence as a concept. For each prediction, the child must give support. For example, if a student says "It's a detective story," ask them to say or point to the evidence that supports their prediction. In this case, the child might say "See the magnifying glass. Detectives use magnifying glasses." Once complete, ask them if they are anxious to see how correct their predictions are. In addition to honing their prediction skills, you will also have created positive anticipation for listening to the entire story! Another pre-reading strategy would be to take a picture walk through the book without reading the text.

2. Briefly check their understanding of the Vocabulary List on the next page (also reproduced on the back cover of the storybook) and clarify if necessary. This may be more necessary with younger age children. You may want to reproduce this page and give it to each child or write on a large chart and discuss together. Conferences could be held with each child later as needed to clarify understanding or the class could participate in a group session to clarify words for everyone.

3. Use your favorite calming exercise to get students ready, quiet and alert before you start to read. Some educators use a certain poem or short song before every read aloud time as a signal for students to be ready to listen.

Note your ideas for getting children ready to listen and be attentive:

____

____

____

____

Understanding Vocabulary

Curious. Being curious means you enjoy finding out the answers to your questions. A curious boy or girl loves to explore for information and will keep digging until they find answers.

Information. Information is what you read, listen to, observe around you, watch on television, or find on the Internet. For example, when you read a book, you learn some facts about the topic of the book. Those facts are information (and you have to check to make sure the "facts" are true).

Research. Research includes all the steps you go through (the process) to find the answer to your information question or problem. To start your research, you must decide on your big topic, narrow it down, and make a plan for how you will find the information you need. After that you can search for your information (see definition of search). Finally, after collecting and organizing what you find, you can present your research. Part of research is also making sure that the information you find can be trusted.

Search. Search means to look for the information you need. For example, you can search for information in books, on the Internet, and by asking for help from your teacher, librarian, or parents. Other words that mean the same as search are *explore* and *investigate*. When you search for information, you learn new things about your topic. Searching is part of the *research* process.

Narrow-down. Let's say that you are working on a school project. Sometimes, you have to "narrow down" a big topic. That means you decide on a *part* of the bigger topic to explore for your project. For example, if you decide on dogs as your big topic, you might want to *narrow it down* to only certain kinds of dogs, like poodles or terriers. If your topic is too big, it will be difficult to handle all the information.

Make a plan. When you "make a plan," you decide where to look for the information you need and who can help you. You also think about ways you might like to present (see definition) your information once you find it.

Brainstorming. When you brainstorm, you try and think of a topic or a question in as many ways as possible.

Facts. When you are positive a piece of information can be proved to be true or correct, it is a fact. Often, you have to check the facts to make sure they are correct.

Predict. Predict means to make a guess about what might happen next. When you read a story, you can predict what might happen next by thinking about the information you already read.

Presenting your research. Presenting means sharing what you learned from your research with others. Sometimes, you will write a report but there are other ways to present your research, too, such as a poster, a diorama, a play, making a book, a PowerPoint presentation and so on.

Reading The Story

While you are reading the story, keep the following in mind:

- An educator's reading aloud to students is an important activity that unfortunately significantly decreases as students learn to read by themselves. How many times have you heard older students read aloud in a monotone fashion? Students need your example even as they become capable of reading on their own. Readers who understand what they are reading are more able to read with intonation and expression. You can help them realize that reading is an active endeavor. The more you become a part of the story, the more you will be able to engage your students in what is actually a very social experience and model that you are understanding what you are reading.

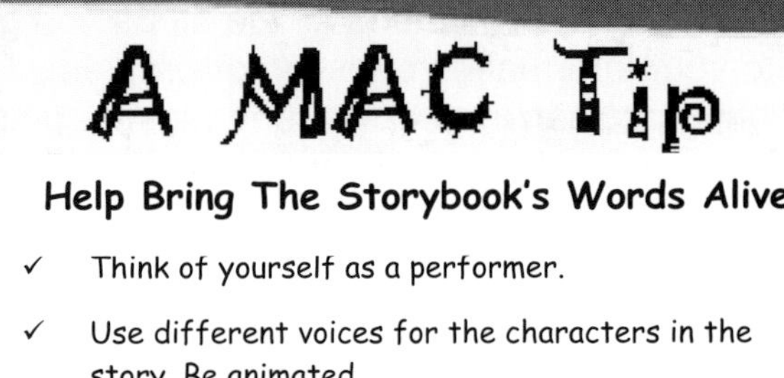

- You should be prepared for and encourage questions that ask for clarification and understanding while you are reading. The supportive environment that you have created will enable this. Don't discourage the questions, answering them as best you can with reference to the story, but quickly returning to the narrative so as not to lose the continuity. Young children often cannot discriminate between a question and a comment or divergent remarks. You may want to discuss this with the children before reading aloud. In any case, do not discourage the children's desire to be active participants in the reading of the story.

- Make the most of the *Interactive Pages*. Encourage question-asking and brainstorming. Help them process the story. Check for comprehension and clarify when necessary. Make sure that all children actively participate activating prior knowledge, if necessary.

Note your ideas for encouraging children to participate:

____

____

____

____

Reinforcing The Learning

Decide how you will reinforce and extend the learning and how you will integrate it into your schedule. This can be accomplished by:

- Immediate follow-up discussion after story
- Related activities such as activity pages, or lesson plans
- Extending the goal of the book (i.e., what are the beginning steps in the research process) to a discussion or unit that includes the during and ending steps in the research process).

Immediate Follow-up

Some of the children may have asked questions as you read the story aloud. By answering those questions and by using the Interactive Pages as periodic check points, you probably have a good idea of their comprehension of the story and its theme. Still, immediate follow-up is a good reinforcer and especially useful for the youngest children. Try some of the following statements and questions as possible discussion starters:

- The Curious Kids have found a caterpillar. They have many important questions about him, but what is the most important question, the BIG QUESTION. Do you remember what it was?
- Mac helps the kids remember the steps for getting started on research; there were three of them. Let's think together about these steps *(i.e., pick a topic or Big Question, narrow it down to smaller questions, make a plan).*
- If you mom or friend asked you what this story was about, what would you tell them? *(Some young children will focus on the squiggly caterpillar or the Curious Kids, but talk with the children until they agree that the story was about how to find the answers to their questions.)*
- End the discussion by asking kids to remember the title of the story. Ask them why they think the title is "The Curious Kids and the SQUIGGLY QUESTION." Why is the question squiggly? Could there be more than one reason?

Related Activities

You can also choose a related activity from Part I of this resource guide. First, decide on when you can accomplish the related activity and how much time you can afford to spend on it. Take a look at these resources and then decide on what types of related activities make sense for you and your students.

Note your ideas for incorporating related activities:

____

____

____

____

Extending the Goal of the Storybook

The goal of the storybook is to introduce information skills needed when *beginning* a research project. You may choose to use the story as a catalyst for an entire unit on caterpillars and butterflies or insects. Such a unit would include the *during* and *ending stage*s of a research project, as well. This resource guide was designed to support all stages of the research process and is separated into sections that address the *beginning, during*, and *ending stage*s of the research process.

To summarize "Making the Most of the Storybook," here's the recipe one more time:

RECIPE

ENHANCING THE LEARNING EXPERIENCE OF READING

THE CURIOUS KIDS AND THE SQUIGGLY QUESTION

1. PLAN (you)
2. PREPARE (students)
3. READ (the story)
4. REINFORCE (learning)

"I'm curious about caterpillars!"

The *Beginning Stage* of the Research Process

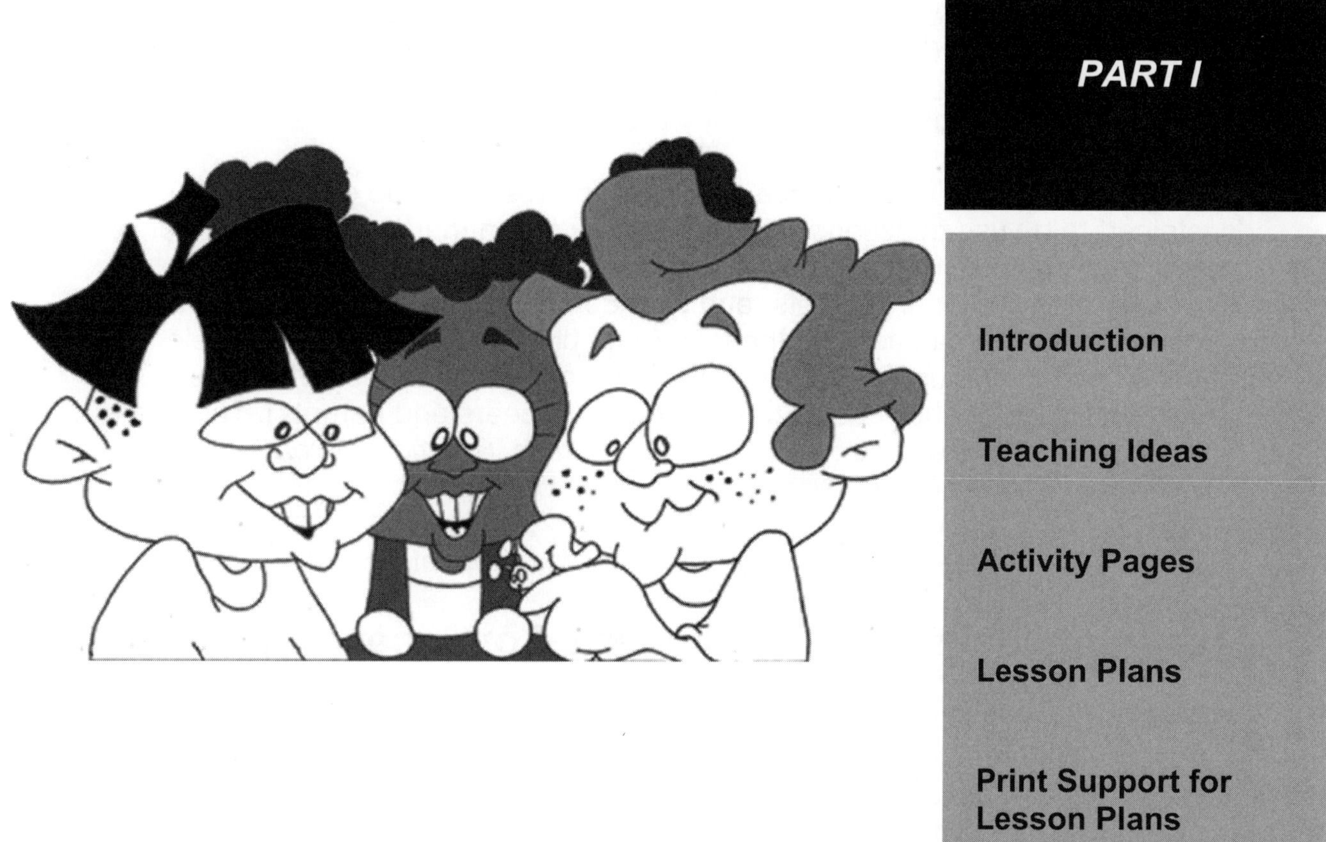

PART I

- **Introduction**
- **Teaching Ideas**
- **Activity Pages**
- **Lesson Plans**
- **Print Support for Lesson Plans**

PART I: THE *BEGINNING STAGE* OF THE RESEARCH PROCESS

Introduction: Think Motivation!

Before proceeding to teaching ideas and lesson plans specific to the information literacy skills and subject area content of the storybook and guide, let's mention a few general yet important motivational principles you should consider. If you also have read *The Strangest Dinosaur That Never Was,* these principles were mentioned in its educators' guide. They are worth repeating.

"In order for learning to take place, students' interest must be gained and sustained (e.g., use questions that arouse curiosity in the *beginning stage* of research). The topic of research must be important to them in some way (e.g., tie research to personal interests, and provide choices for topics). They must feel confident that they can achieve the task (e.g., break tasks into manageable chunks), and they must find satisfaction in the end result of their efforts (e.g., provide a forum for showcasing their research to peers and parents). These are just a few ideas to start with. You can find others in *Turning Kids on to Research: The Power of Motivation* published by Libraries Unlimited."

– *The Strangest Dinosaur That Never Was: Educators' Guide*, 2003, p.21

Teaching Ideas (for getting started on research)

We will present teaching ideas and sample activities in an encapsulated lesson plan format in order to provide as many as possible. Later in Part I, we will present two fully described lesson plans for this stage of research with print support materials. There are a number of library media specialists and classroom teachers whose lesson plans have stimulated many of the following ideas. We will credit them as we go along. Feel free to pick and choose as many teaching ideas as you think you need to introduce the *beginning stage* of research. Or use the suggested ideas as a springboard for your own creativity in developing ideas that meet your specific curriculum requirements. While the topic here is caterpillars and butterflies, you can easily adapt the teaching ideas to other insects and/or other topics your students may be studying. Each teaching idea cites the national information literacy standard(s) addressed. You can read more about these standards in *Information Power: Building Partnerships for Learning* published by the American Library Association (1998). As mentioned in the introduction, please refer to the Mid-continent Research for Education and Learning (McREL) national content standards (www.mcrel.org) for each subject area and standard cited.

The first two teaching ideas address basic comprehension of the storybook. The story web or story map described in the first activity is an excellent way to evaluate whether students have comprehended the text (In Part 3, you will also see how effective a story web can be as a culminating activity). You may notice that a number of teaching ideas provide at least some degree of choice even if it is only reaching into a mystery box to select a butterfly cutout with the name of the butterfly to be researched. Choice affects motivation to learn in a positive way by adding relevance to the topic of research.

1	**Title**: Using a Story Web to Retell "The Curious Kids and the Squiggly Question" (K-3)
	Learning Objective(s): Students demonstrate comprehension of the storybook by recalling and retelling the story in their own words.
	What to Do: Enlarge the activity sheet (included under *Activity Pages for Teaching Ideas*) entitled "Using a Story Web to Retell the Story," mount it on a poster board and place on an easel. Pointing to the oval with the title and author's name, ask students why the author might have given the book that title. What did she mean by the "Squiggly Question?" Have children retell the story using the story elements from the poster as a guide. As they retell, fill in the rectangles for setting, characters, problems and solutions that web out from the title/author oval. It is not necessary to make a point of the sequence. Students should be naturally addressing the story elements as they retell. If they get stuck, prompt them with questions like "What were the Curious Kids concerned about?" If they respond that the Curious Kids were worried about what Squiggly should eat, acknowledge it as one of the "problems" and fill in that section of the poster. Make certain they realize that the solutions include having the research/information skills to know how to ask the right questions, plan where to find the information, and as the story concludes – putting their plan into action.
	Standards Addressed: **Information Power**: Derives meaning from information presented creatively in a variety of formats (5.2) **Subject Area(s)**: Language Arts (Level 1) 5.0, 5.4; 7.3

2	**Title**: From Story Comprehension to Higher Order Thinking (2-3)
	Learning Objective(s): After recalling information (including the vocabulary list) from *The Curious Kids and the Squiggly Question,* students can generalize the use of research skills to everyday life.
	What to Do: Review the vocabulary list of words used in the story (see *Introduction*) You will have already introduced the list prior to reading the story aloud. Challenge students by asking them how much they remember about the story. Use the story comprehension activity sheet entitled "How Much Do You Remember?" as a starter (included under *Activity Pages for Teaching Ideas*). Once you are confident they comprehend the story, use the book as a springboard to engage higher order thinking skills. Brainstorm with students asking questions like "Why do you suppose it is important that you should learn research skills?" "How can having these skills help you in everyday life?"
	Standards Addressed: **Information Power**: Integrates new information into one's own knowledge (3.2); Applies information in critical thinking and problem solving (3.3) **Subject Area**: Language Arts (Level 1) 7.1, 7.5; (Level 2) 7.5, 7.6

The next activities help reinforce information skills for the *beginning stage* of research that were introduced in the storybook.

3	**Title**: From BIG TOPIC or BIG QUESTION to Little Questions
	Learning Objectives: Students practice the skills introduced in the storybook of 1) brainstorming and 2) narrowing down the topic.
	What to Do: Create a colorful K-W-L chart decorated with caterpillar and butterfly drawings or clipart and a cutout of Squiggly. At the top of the chart write "Big topic or question: Caterpillars" and leave the rest blank. Introduce the activity: "In the story, the Curious Kids brainstormed what they already knew about caterpillars. Let's practice brainstorming and try and think of all the things we already know about them and I will write them down." After brainstorming, remind students that they already have their big topic which is… (they will yell out "caterpillars!") Now, it is time for them to narrow down their topic by thinking of questions *they* want to answer and write their questions in the W column of the chart. Encourage students to add new questions to the chart that the Curious Kids didn't ask. This may be a good way to get them thinking about caterpillars turning into different types of butterflies. Some may want to research the Monarch butterfly or other types. Some may wish to explore what caterpillars like to eat (See "Chomp! Chomp! What Do Caterpillars Like to Eat?" provided under *Activity Pages for Teaching Ideas*). You can return to the KWL in the *during* and *ending stage*s of research.

<table>
<tr><td></td><td>Standards Addressed:
    Information Power: Formulates questions based on information needs (1.3)
    Subject Area: Science 4.2</td></tr>
<tr><td></td><td>Comments:
1. Use this activity to reinforce the interactive page discussion in the storybook (p.17). Since this activity involves actually seeing their ideas written on the K-W-L chart and generating new ideas, it serves as an excellent follow-up.
2. The cutout of Squiggly that you can color in and use on chart and the butterfly cutouts are included under Activity Pages for Teaching Ideas.
3. Use the "Chomp! Chomp! What Do Caterpillars Like to Eat?" for students who have identified this area as a question to explore.</td></tr>
</table>

<table>
<tr><td>4</td><td>Title: My Research Questions and Plan (1 – 3)</td></tr>
<tr><td></td><td>Learning Objective(s): Students can articulate their research questions and make a preliminary plan.</td></tr>
<tr><td></td><td>What to Do: As a follow-up to teaching idea #3, have students use the activity sheet "My Research Questions and Plan" (included under Activity Pages for Teaching Ideas) to choose their individual research questions. You may wish to refer back to the K-W-L chart as a reminder of some of the questions already brainstormed as a group. This activity should also reinforce the planning aspect of research introduced in the storybook. Using some of the cues provided on the activity sheet, students can think about where they might search for information. If this is already decided, have students circle the resources you wish them to use, or write them in the space provided. Planning also includes thinking ahead to how the research might be presented once complete. If students are given a choice, they can use the sheet to tell how they plan to present. For younger students, the presentation format may already be decided by you and that information can simply be entered on their sheet. Have students refer back to their plan from time to time to make sure they are staying on track. Of course, there is always the possibility that a new or related question may arise from their initial search. If possible, allow for some flexibility.</td></tr>
<tr><td></td><td>Standards Addressed:
    Information Power: Formulates questions based on information needs (1.3); Identifies a variety of potential sources of information (1.4)
    Subject Area: Language Arts (Level 1) 4.1, 4.2; (Level 2); 4.1</td></tr>
</table>

5	**Title**: Fiction or Nonfiction: Exploring Images (K-2)
	Learning Objective(s): Students can identify when an image represents something fictional or nonfictional.
	What to Do: This activity is helpful in the "beginning" stage of research as students consider different resources for finding answers to their research questions and the verity of each. It will also be helpful later as they explore and evaluate information. A fun way to introduce fiction vs. nonfiction is to create a PowerPoint presentation (or poster) that includes clipart of animals in real vs. exaggerated situations. Students will enjoy brainstorming 'which is which' and trying to convince you of their arguments. To relate this lesson plan suggestion to the storybook, use the activity sheet entitled "Meet Squiggly's Friend Squirmy: Fiction or Nonfiction?" (included under *Activity Pages for Teaching Ideas*).
	Standards Addressed: **Information Power**: Evaluates information critically and competently (2.0) **Subject Area**: Language Arts 4.0, 4.2; 5.4; Thinking and Reasoning, 3.0, 6.0
	Comments: Michele Messenger inspired the above teaching idea. Her graphic images of both fiction and nonfiction include real pictures of nonfiction topics, cartoon pictures of nonfiction, silly drawings of fiction and realistic looking but fictional situations. According to Michele, "One of the neatest side effects of this lesson is that they [students] go around in the library and, I'm told, in the classroom for days saying 'This is fiction, this in nonfiction.'"

8	**Title**: True or False: What do You Think?
	Learning Objective(s): 1. Children make educated guesses about statements they will later prove or disprove. 2. Students practice planning skills.
	What to Do: Create a handout for K-1 students with instructions that you read. For grades 2 and 3, include more text on their reading levels. On the handout, include both true and false statements about caterpillars and butterflies. Using their prior knowledge and/or intuition, each student is given a choice of one or two statements to prove or disprove (i.e., hypothesizing for primary students). Guide students as they consider whether statements have inaccurate or possibly misleading information. Their predictions can form the basis of the smaller research questions they will investigate in the *during stage* of research. Follow-up as a whole class, practicing planning skills by brainstorming which resources would be appropriate for locating information to prove or disprove their predictions.
	Standards Addressed: **Information Power**: Identifies inaccurate or misleading information (2.3); Identifies a variety of potential sources of information (1.4). **Subject Area**: Thinking and Reasoning (Level 1) 1.2.

In addition to the above teaching ideas, there are others that would also be appropriate for the *beginning stage* of research. For example, consider demonstrating a child-friendly search engine like Yahooligans or Kids Click to teach students about keywords and how they can be used to help narrow down their topics.

Activity Pages for Teaching Ideas

In the next section, you will find a number of activity pages that can be used to support the above teaching ideas.

Using a Story Web To Retell the Story

Story Comprehension

How Much Do You Remember?

See how many questions you can answer about *The Curious Kids and the Squiggly Question*! If you need help, check Mac's clues at the bottom of the page.

1. Timmy, Chen, and Tanisha slid down the slippery ____________________ at the school playground.

2. The Curious Kids got their nickname because they were always ________________ about something.

3. At the playground, Timmy found a ____________________________.

4. Tanisha wondered how long it takes for a caterpillar to become a ____________________.

5. Timmy's question was "How do we keep Squiggly _____________ until he becomes a butterfly?"

6. They decided they did not know enough about caterpillars. To save Squiggly they would need more ____________________.

7. Mac, Information _________________, gave them clues to help with their research. The first clue was "Pick a topic or a ___________________." The second clue was "______________ it down" by thinking of smaller questions. The third clue was "Make a _____________."

8. At the end of the story, Mac fluffed up his cape and ___________ into the air!

Check out these clues!

Detective	alive	information	leaped
question	butterfly	down	curious
plan	caterpillar	slide	

Chomp! Chomp! What do Caterpillars Like to Eat?

Caterpillars can be very fussy eaters. Use your information detective skills to find out who likes to eat what!

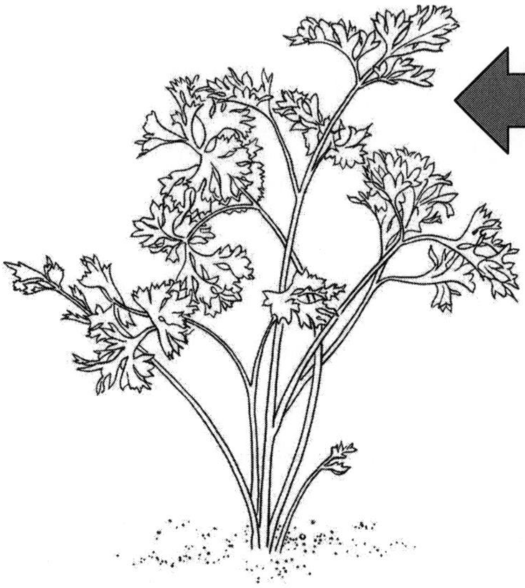

This is parsley. Find out which caterpillar(s) like parsley. Write your discoveries below.

____

____

This is Queen Ann's Lace. Find out which caterpillar(s) likes this plant. Write your discoveries below.

____

____

This is milkweed. Find out who likes to eat milkweed and <u>only</u> milkweed. Write your discovery below.

____

____

Squiggly for Cutting or Coloring

Butterflies for
Cutting or
Coloring

My Research Question(s) and Plan

Your **BIG topic** is caterpillars. Now you can **narrow down** your topic to some smaller questions you could research. In the space below, write one or more of the smaller research questions you will explore.

My research question(s):

____

____

____

My plan: Think of where you might **search** for the information you need. Circle the sources you plan to use to answer your research questions. Then, add any more you can think of on the blank line.

Science Magazine **Books on butterflies** **Internet**

Encyclopedia **Observe with my own eyes** **Experiment**

Visit a butterfly garden or farm **Online catalog**

Any other ideas? Write them here: __________________________

Part of your plan is thinking about how you will **present** your research once you are finished. How will you present your research? Write your idea below.

____

Complete Lesson Plans

The following pages contain two fully described lesson plans and print support materials. Both lessons can be part of a larger unit on insects. They combine activities that occur both in the *beginning* and *during stage*s of research. Rather than saving the nature hike for the "during" stage of research, it is used at the beginning to get students excited about selecting their research topic!

Lesson Plan Title:
Going on a Bug Hunt

Created by: Sharon Coatney

Stage of Research:	Beginning (also includes some "during" research activities)
Grade Levels:	2,3
Time Required:	This is a week's worth of 1 hour a day science periods or could be structured with a ½ day nature activity and then 2 hours of follow up classroom work. Time may vary according to the ages of the children.
Comments/Notes:	Students really enjoy this project. It needs to be done in the early fall or in the spring when weather permits. If possible, locate a farm or a park or other nature area that will allow students to collect specimens in various habitats (in a wooded area, near a pond, open field etc). Make sure that group leaders help students choose what is safe to collect (i.e. dead specimens, live insects that are not dangerous-no wasps, bumblebees, etc.)
Information Literacy Standards:	Recognizes the need for information (1.1); Formulates questions based on information needs (1.3); Develops and uses successful strategies for locating information (1.5)
Related Subject Area(s) and National Content Standards: (McREL standards)	Science: 6.0 Language Arts: 4.0
Learning Goals/Objectives:	1. Students will find and choose the insect that they want to research. 2. Students will determine and describe the attributes of their insect. 3. Students will list the questions they want to answer. 4. Students will find the answers to their questions (in the ***during stage*** of research).

Required Materials:	Parent or older student helpers to lead groups; digital cameras (optional), butterfly nets, collection jars with lids, books and magazines to complete the research project. Student clipboards, worksheets, pencils, and drawing materials.
Procedures:	**BEGINNING RESEARCH:** Take students on a nature hike. Divide students into groups to explore the type of habitat available (water areas, open fields, wooded areas, etc.) Each student will capture and /or take a digital picture of at least one insect that they want to find out about. Students will fill out a "Bug Identity Sheet" (included under *Print Support Materials for Lesson Plans* at the end of Part 1) listing what they already know about the insect (physical characteristics, habitat where found, etc.) to determine the attributes of their insect. This will enable them to determine if they have captured an insect or a spider and answer some basic observable questions. Students will be able to add their own questions to the bug identity sheet. **DURING RESEARCH:** With the aide of teachers and parents, students will peruse Web sites, books and other information sources to determine the name of their insect. If digital pictures are taken, students can complete the assignment over time at school. A fun way to do this activity is to schedule a day outside with students, bring the "bug books and other print sources" with you and do the research in the natural environment.
Learning Assessment(s):	Students will be able to explain their plan for research.

Lesson Plan Title:
Being the Bug

Created by: Sharon Coatney

Stage of Research:	Beginning (with some "during" research suggestions)
Grade Levels:	2,3
Time Required:	1 week of science periods
Comments/Notes:	This lesson could ultimately encompass all stages of the research process.
Information Literacy Standards:	Formulates questions based on information needs (1.3); Organizes information for practical application (3.1)
Related Subject Area(s) and National Content Standards: (McREL standards)	Language Arts: 1.0; 4.0; 7.0 Science: 6.0
Learning Goals/Objectives:	1.Students will choose a bug to research and portray in a classroom production. 2. Students will read and listen to stories, taking notes to determine personal choice. 3. Students will note new vocabulary words for further study.
Required Materials:	-Books and stories featuring bugs as the main characters (i.e.-The Very Hungry Caterpillar, by Eric Carle; Bubba and Trixie by Lisa Campbell Ernst, selected Aesops Fables) -Encyclopedias, basic bug books, dictionaries, the Web
Procedures:	**BEGINNING RESEARCH:** Over a period of 1 week, students will listen to and read several stories. Given a notetaking sheet ("Bug Words"-provided under *Print Support Materials for Lesson Plans*), students will note new vocabulary and things they want to know about each bug portrayed in the story. At the end of the week students will choose from the sheets to determine which bug they want to portray in the class portrayal/parade. Tell students that they will eventually dress up like this bug and write a short script describing themselves. This script will be presented to their class and they will participate in a bug parade throughout the school. They will need to become an expert about their bug. Using their note sheets, have students formulate questions in order to make a research plan.

	DURING RESEARCH: Have students scan the information available in encyclopedias, books and on the Web to help determine if sufficient information will be available to find the answers they will need to complete their plan. For instance, perhaps the bug in the story is not easily definable, or is in fact fictional.
Learning Assessment(s):	Students will make a personal choice based on notes taken from listening and reading and a quick scan of the basic resources available to them.

Print Support Materials for Lesson Plans

The reproducible "Bug Identity Sheet" and the "Bug Words Note Sheet" on the following pages support the above lesson plans.

Bug Identity Sheet

1 My Observations

How many legs? _____ How many body parts?_____ Wings?(Yes or No) ______

What colors?______________________ Body Markings?(Yes or No) ____________

How does he move? ______________ What does he eat?_____________________

Where did you find him? ____

Draw a picture of your bug here!

2 What Do You Want to Know?

List your questions below

3 Where Did I Find My Information?

Check off and write title or name of source

☐ **BOOK** ______________________

☐ **MAGAZINE** ___________________

☐ **WEB** ________________________

☐ **OBSERVATION** ________________

☐ **INTERVIEW** __________________

☐ **OTHER** ______________________

Bug Words Note Sheet

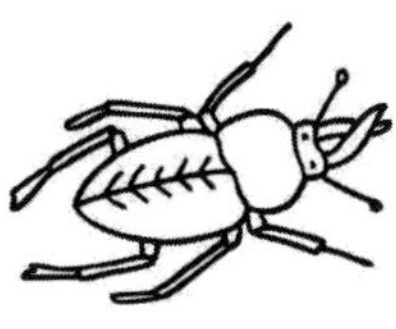

Write your bug words in the first space in each box. Write your notes in the larger space below. Later, you will choose the bug you wish to portray!

MY BUG CHOICE IS

____

"I will be an expert on my bug!"

"Look what I found out!"

The *During Stage* of the Research Process

PART II

Introduction

Teaching Ideas

Activity Pages

Lesson Plans

Print Support for Lesson Plans

PART II: THE *DURING STAGE* OF THE RESEARCH PROCESS

Introduction

While *The Curious Kids and the Squiggly Question* focused only on the *beginning stage* of research, in Parts 2 and 3 of this guide, we will continue with caterpillars and butterflies (or insects in general) as a topic and suggest teaching ideas for the *during* and *ending stage*s of the research process.

Students should understand that research is kind of messy and it doesn't always proceed in a linear fashion. We say the *during stage* of research but research is not actually a linear process; students may have to revisit their original questions or narrow down their questions even more. As mentioned earlier, students at this stage of the process may also become frustrated as they explore and find so much information. Kuhlthau refers to this as uncertainty. Once resolved, the confidence level increases.

The following pages describe a number of teaching ideas for the *during stage* of research.

Teaching Ideas (for the during stage of research)

1	**Title**: Dictionaries Versus Encyclopedias
	Learning Objective(s): 1. Students will compare and contrast dictionaries and encyclopedias. 2. Students will discriminate between dictionary entries and encyclopedia entries. 3. Students will determine the uses appropriate for each type of reference source.
	What to Do: 1. Using an overhead transparency, show students a dictionary entry about caterpillars. Together list the attributes and uses of this type of entry. 2. Using an overhead transparency, show students an encyclopedia entry about caterpillars (or an insect). Together list the attributes and uses of this type of entry. 3. Using a Venn diagram (provided under *Activity Pages to Support Teaching Ideas*), determine the common attributes and uses of these two types of entries. 4. Give students scenarios such as: Your teacher has given you an assignment to find out what the word habitat means. Which resource might you use to find a quick answer? You would like to find out some beginning but general information about the monarch butterfly but you don't have time to read an entire book on it. What resource might you use? You can create other scenarios. 5. Have students discuss these scenarios in small groups and then come back together to check their understanding.
	Standards Addressed: **Information Power**: Evaluates information critically and competently (2.0) **Subject Area**: Thinking and Reasoning 3.2 (Level 1); 3.2 (Level 2)
	Comments: The ability to discriminate between the use of dictionaries, and encyclopedias is very difficult for young children and is often a tested item on standardized tests.

2	**Title**: Introduction to Dewey: Where Would Squiggly Go?
	Learning Objective(s): Students will understand that the Dewey numbers on nonfiction books "mean something," representing the content or ideas found in the book.
	What to Do: This delightful activity is a great introduction to the Dewey Decimal System and is fully described in the lesson plan at the conclusion of Part 2.
	Standards Addressed: See lesson plan by Michele Messenger at the end of Part 2.

<table>
<tr><td rowspan="5">3</td><td>Title: The Changing Faces of Caterpillars (K-2)</td></tr>
<tr><td>Learning Objective(s): Students explore the library and learn about metamorphosis in their travels.</td></tr>
<tr><td>What to Do: Props are fun! This idea can be used to maintain interest levels of K-2 students in the during stage of research as they learn about metamorphosis. LMS will pack a suitcase with exciting items such as a safari hat, binoculars, magnifying glass, butterfly net, notetaking journal, etc. When students arrive to the library media center, explore the contents of the suitcase with them. Have them imagine what these items could be used for. Eventually, let them know that these are items they might use in researching the different stages of a butterfly's life. Students' enthusiasm will continue to be heightened as they begin a three-day journey in the library. Set up the library with teacher-made paper trees and shrubbery throughout. On and around the trees and shrubs, use magazine or computer graphics depicting various stages including eggs, caterpillars, pupas and butterflies. Allow students to "travel" with a partner to collect samples and discuss their findings. With guidance from the LMS, each team will explore nonfiction resources to gather facts.</td></tr>
<tr><td>Standards Addressed:
Information Power: Identifies a variety of potential sources of information (1.4); Develops and uses successful strategies for locating information.
Subject Area: Science/Life Sciences 4.2</td></tr>
<tr><td>Comments: Karen Leo created this teaching idea.</td></tr>
</table>

<table>
<tr><td rowspan="5">4</td><td>Title: Be an Information Detective!</td></tr>
<tr><td>Learning Objective(s): Students evaluate Web pages to determine whether the information on their caterpillar, butterfly, or insect seems factual, up-to-date, comprehensive (enough information), etc.</td></tr>
<tr><td>What to Do: Create two HTML pages for your library media center. Make one have exaggerated claims, like caterpillars eat more than 50 pounds of leaves a day. Ask children to think about it. Does this seem true? Why or why not? Ask students if they can believe everything they find on the Internet? What should they look for? Have students explore one or more authentic Web sites that you have book marked. Use the "Be an Information Detective" activity sheet (included under Activity Pages to Support Teaching Ideas) to help guide them in their evaluation.</td></tr>
<tr><td>Standards Addressed:
Information Power: Evaluates information critically and competently (2.0); Distinguishes among fact, point of view, and opinion (3.2); Identifies inaccurate and misleading information (3.3); Selects information appropriate to the problem or question at hand (3.4)
Subject Area: Technology (Level 1) 6.4</td></tr>
<tr><td>Comments: This activity really makes children feel they are playing the part of an information detective!</td></tr>
</table>

5	**Title**: Notetaking for Understanding (2-3)
	Learning Objective(s): Students practice notetaking skills.
	What to Do: Copy a paragraph on caterpillars or other bug from a reference, create an overhead transparency or incorporate it into a computer-based presentation. Project it for the class to see. Model (using a talk aloud approach) reading a paragraph, then removing it from the screen. Have large chart paper nearby where you can create a graphic organizer such a web or concept map to demonstrate notetaking. Add a few keywords and phrases in your own words. Let students know you are putting your notes into your own words. Bring the paragraph back on screen and model re-checking it to make sure that your note was accurate and complete enough. Add a bit more to your notes. Check again. Re-read your notes out loud to see if you can explain what you read with your notes. Now, use another excerpt from a resource and let students practice as a group. The idea is for them to realize that they must take good enough notes to make sense of them after the fact. Eventually bring in the other aspects of notetaking such as using quotations around words that are copied exactly. Skimming, skanning, extracting, and crediting the source are also part of learning how to take good notes. For novelty, you could create an Information Detective Log Book just for taking notes!
	Standards Addressed: **Information Power**: Organizes information for practical application (3.1); Integrates new information into one's own knowledge (3.2). **Subject Area**: Language Arts (Reading-Level 1) 5.4; (Reading Level 2) 5.3, 5.9.
	Comments: Learning good notetaking skills may be of some help in addressing a common student problem that begins early on. That problem is difficulty re-telling (in their own words) what they have read in a way that demonstrates an accurate understanding of the content. Often they will include information not even contained in the reading or contradicted in the reading. While able to read aloud accurately, for many students it often isn't sinking in. If concerned about an explanation generated by a student, ask the child to explain where the information was found. You may also need to have the child show you where the book or resource makes a similar statement. Modeling good notetaking skills may help.

6	**Title**: Raising Squiggly: The Real Thing
	Learning Objective(s): 1) Students will practice a range of information literacy skills throughout the project including location, collection (notetaking), and organization. 2) Students will be able to identify and sequence the lifecycle stages of a butterfly.
	What to Do: Children put on their junior information detective caps in this teaching idea that spans several weeks. They will experience first-hand the lifecycle of a butterfly. This teaching idea is fully described in the lesson of the same title at the conclusion of Part 2.
	Standards Addressed: (See related lesson plan later in Part 2)

The ideas above are a good starting place for information literacy lessons on the topic of caterpillars and butterflies or insects that are appropriate for the *during stage* of research. There are many more you could explore. For example, have students learn about the atlas as they study the Monarch butterfly's long journey north from Mexico. This idea could be integrated with math as students determine how far the Monarch butterfly must travel. Older students may enjoy learning about the World Almanac for Kids and searching for interesting facts using the table of contents and the index. Even at this early stage, students should also learn how to give credit for the sources of the information they find and use. In the early grades, that can be as simple as noting the title of a book and its author, the name of a Web site, and the title of a reference book with its volume and page number.

Activity Pages for Teaching Ideas

In the next section, you will find two activity pages that can be used to support several of the above teaching ideas.

Can be used with teaching idea #1 and to compare and contrast insects.

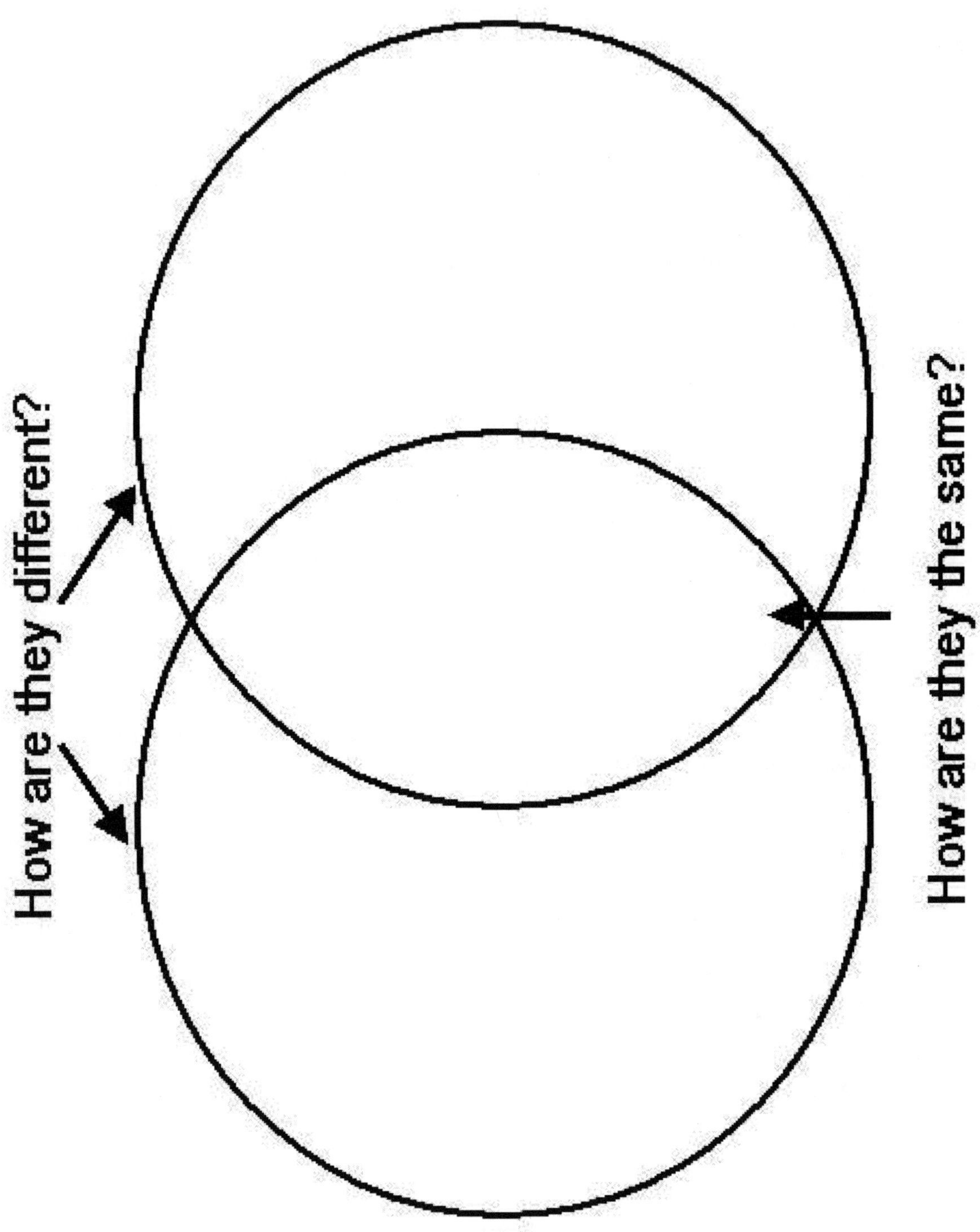

Be An Information Detective!

Some Web sites are good ones. Some are poor ones. Others just need some improvement. Use your skills and the checklist below to investigate a Web site about caterpillars and butterflies or insects. Your teacher or librarian will help you choose one. Answer the questions by putting a checkmark or an "X" in the YES or NO boxes.

YES	NO	
☐	☐	Do you think the information is factual? (The word factual means true.)
☐	☐	Is there enough of the information you need?
☐	☐	Is the information up-to-date?
☐	☐	Does everything on the Web site work the way it should? (For example, do the links all work? Is it easy to find your way around?)
☐	☐	Is there a way to contact the author of the Web site?

If most of the answers are **YES**, this site passes your inspection!

Lesson Plans

The following lesson contributed by creative school library media specialist, Michele Messenger, is ideal for the *during stage* of research in which students practice skills for locating and accessing information. This makes learning the Dewey Decimal System a fun experience for primary grade students.

Lesson Plan Title:
Introduction to Dewey: Where Would Squiggly Go?

Created by: Michele Messenger

Stage of Research:	During
Grade Levels:	1, 2
Time Required:	1 –2 sessions
Comments/Notes:	This lesson is designed for students who are first being introduced to the Dewey Decimal System of classification for nonfiction books. It should be used after students have an understanding of the difference between fiction and nonfiction. (See the fiction/nonfiction teaching idea suggested for the *Beginning stage* of research, Part I)
Information Literacy Standards:	Accesses information efficiently and effectively (1.0); Recognizes the need for information (1.1)
Related Subject Area(s) and National Content Standards: (McREL standards)	Thinking and Reasoning: 2.0; 3.0; 5.0; 6.0
Learning Goals/Objectives:	Students will understand that the Dewey numbers on nonfiction books "mean something," representing the content or ideas found in the book. Students will be able to: 1. understand that each Dewey number has a meaning and is not just randomly assigned. 2. match the house number in their hands to the general spot in their school libraries nonfiction collection. 3. take the knowledge learned through this activity and begin to apply it by noticing what hundred some of their favorite subjects are located in **Ex: caterpillar – 500.**
Required Materials:	Larger signs in the shape of a leaf that name each hundred as a town. Names should apply to the content. Ex: 600s could be Technology Town - population 600

	Sturdy paper Squiggly cards (graphics provided under *Print Support Materials for Lesson Plan*), large enough to see at a distance. Each should have an address printed on it. Ex: 636 Dog Drive or 612 Body Boulevard
Procedures:	1. As a class the students will sit in the nonfiction area that has been clearly defined to them. They will be reminded that most nonfiction books are informational resources with true facts in them. 2. Excitedly ask the class if they know how the numbers get on the books call number sticker. Explain what a call number is. 3. Tell them about the Dewey Decimal System (DDS) and a bit about before it was used and the way books were arranged and found. 4. Ask them to think of their own address and turn and whisper it to their neighbor. Then ask anyone with a very descriptive street name to share the name and, if known, how the street got that name. If the reason is not known, have the class brainstorm ways the street could have gotten that name, for example Cherry Tree Lane having cherry trees along, behind, or above it. This works best with older students who know their address. 5. Tell the students that the DDS is broken into the hundreds and that you are going to begin an exciting journey learning about those numbers by taking a trip through the hundreds towns. 6. Walk around your nonfiction section placing the Town Signs on the shelving, reading each one. Point out that each town has a population such as Technology Town - pop. 600 (because it is the 600s). (The population is just an additional cue for students.) 7. Next tell the students that they will each get the chance to place one (or more) Squiggly cards in the town where they belong by matching the address on their Squiggly card to the town name, population, and/or any signage that already exists in your library media center. 8. Choose a rather attentive and previously successful child to go first, but ask them if they mind going first. Then just go around the group in order of the way they are sitting. My students are at tables, surrounded by a U of nonfiction books which lends itself perfectly to just go on to the next table. 9. Remind the student looking that they can get help if

	needed and also remind the spectators of their responsibilities, that help is only help if you want it and that it is always hardest when it is your turn! Try to give the struggling students numbers that are more obvious, close to them or have been done just a few seconds ago. Give the more confident students the first used number. Always remember to read all of the house numbers out loud. Second graders are reading at such a wide range of levels, it gives more confidence instantly, especially since, to make the activity most meaningful, some semi-technical terms will be used.
Learning Assessment(s):	Students will be assessed at the time of their activity. Successfully placing their Squiggly card in the correct hundred shows that they were listening, following directions and grasping the concept of the lesson. Furthermore, watching students choose nonfiction books directly after this lesson will show you how much they absorbed because of the way they look with newly educated eyes.

Print Support Materials for Lesson Plan

Reproducible Squiggly cards for marking addresses for the above lesson can be found on the next page.

Introduction to Dewey: Where Would Squiggly Go?

Reproduce these Squiggly cutouts for students. Print a house address on each one as suggested in the associated lesson plan by Michele Messenger.

Lesson Plan Title:
Raising Squiggly: The Real Thing

Created by: Marilyn Arnone and Inspired by Many

Stage of Research:	During
Grade Levels:	K-3
Time Required:	Two to three weeks depending on your caterpillar
Comments/Notes:	This lesson takes place after students have already done some preliminary research in the LMC. From the dictionary activity early on they will know the meaning of the word habitat. Students will feel like real Junior Information Detectives just like the Curious Kids from the storybook.
Information Literacy Standards:	Develops and uses successful strategies for locating information (1.5); Selects information appropriate to the problem or question at hand (2.4); Organizes information for practical application (3.1); Integrates new information into one's own knowledge.
Related Subject Area(s) and National Content Standards: (McREL standards)	Science (Life Sciences) 6.0 Language Arts (Writing) 4.0
Learning Goals/Objectives:	1. Students will practice a range of information literacy skills throughout the project. 2. Students will be able to identify and sequence the lifecycle stages of a butterfly. 3. Students will observe behaviors and use a log to record their findings.
Required Materials:	Detective log (provided under *Print Support Materials for Lesson Plan*) or diaries Larvae (either that you find or from butterfly kit) Digital camera or camcorder Materials to create a habitat (described later) Larval food (e.g., plants that your type of caterpillar eats) Magnifying glass Reference materials *Procedures continued on next page….*

Procedures:

Photo 1: Building a habitat

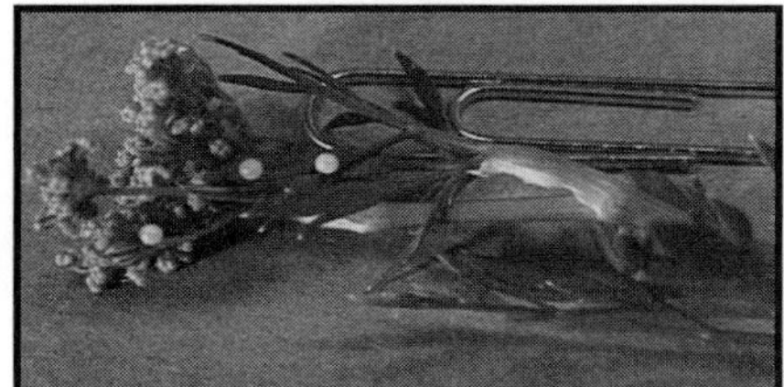
Photo 2: Observing the size of eggs next to a paper clip

Photo 3: Observing that the tiny caterpillar has a white band around its middle. He will go through several big changes.

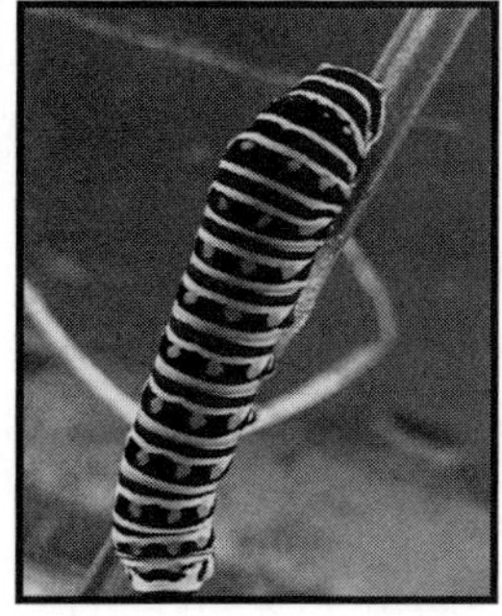
Photo 4: Observing another growth stage of the caterpillar

1. Create a habitat. It could be made out of a shoebox, a large jar, or even an old aquarium that is no longer being used. Cover the opening with netting. I used a long forgotten aquarium and turned it on its side for easy access (see Photo 1). The habitat will need to be kept clean of droppings. Using paper towels to absorb moisture also helped a lot. Include some sticks that caterpillars can attach themselves to when they reach the chrysalis (pupa) stage.
2. If possible, take children on a field trip to a butterfly farm, butterfly garden, or a place you know for sure attracts butterflies. Make sure you have enough helpers. To make it fun, bring a magnifying glass. Put your detective caps on and start looking for caterpillar eggs! They are tiny so everyone will have to look carefully.
3. Have students use their detective log to practice notetaking skills either by writing (older children) or drawing pictures of their observations (K-1). This can include notes about where they found eggs, what type of food they observed caterpillars eating, and general observations about caterpillar and butterfly behaviors. (Alternatively, you can purchase a butterfly kit but the above is more fun!) Collect enough larvae so that hopefully you will have at least one egg that makes it to the butterfly stage (butterfly kits generally include about four). The next step is for students to raise their own little Squiggly back in the classroom or LMC! And his home is ready!
4. Students (with your guidance) will have noted the type of food (plant) that the caterpillars (who were on the same plants as the eggs) ate. Have a good supply of that in the habitat. (we were raising Black Swallowtails who were partial to parsley and they went through lots of plants)
5. Over the next few weeks, the students will delight in their observations. They will witness first hand the lifecycle of a butterfly. Capture it all with a digital still camera or video camcorder. If you use a camcorder, it is fun to record children's reflections along the way. Using a simple editing program, you can delight them at the end with a video that encapsulates the whole experience!

Photo 5: Observing and recording how much food a caterpillar can eat in a day!

Photo 6: Big discovery! Caterpillars respond to sound, especially to low voices. Look at those horns!

Photo 7: Now a fully formed chrysalis.

Photo 8: A beautiful butterfly has emerged! Should we change its name now?!

Prepare students that while they are going to witness the entire lifecycle they may miss some of the transitions. For example, we never really saw the caterpillar emerge from its egg. It was already a tiny speck of a caterpillar the next time we observed! The same thing goes for witnessing the many instars (changes like shedding skin or technically its exoskeleton).

6. The curriculum related information literacy activities are plentiful. Let's start with science.

- Using their own observations (and notes) as a trigger, guide students in the LMC through the processes of exploring, collecting, and organizing information to find out answers to all their "why" questions. Here are some you will hear:
    - Why did Squiggly (or whatever name chosen) have a white band around him and then today he doesn't? (See Photo 3)
    - Why is he black and yellow and has polka dots all over him? (Good opportunity to look into ways insects protect themselves, look scary, etc.)
    - How come the dots looked like dots before and now they are mushing together? (Compare Photos 4 and 5)
    - Why does he sometimes eat a lot of food and then he slows down?

Perhaps you will capture their unexpected discoveries on videotape (See Photo 6)!

Collaborating with the classroom teacher, students can learn about metamorphosis and the sequence of the four stages of a butterfly's life. They can utilize charts, bar graphs, graphic organizers and other tools in their hands-on research to predict, measure, record, and discuss their findings. You can introduce diaries and/or use their detective logs to tie in with language arts. You can tie into any number of art projects. And then there's the payoff—a beautiful butterfly or perhaps more than one if you are lucky! (See Part III for ideas on presenting their research.)

Learning Assessment(s):	Assessments will vary depending on your focus. Some may include: -Can they correctly sequence the stages of a butterfly's life? Know parts of a caterpillar? etc. -Are they able to find (with guidance) information related to their observations and questions in the encyclopedia, online catalog, books, and other resources you demonstrated? -Can the younger students convey their observations either in pictures or words? -Were there meaningful entries in the older students' detective logs? -Were students enthusiastic about doing the research? Did their confidence about engaging in research increase? (motivational assessments, technically, but nonetheless important)

Print Support Materials for Lesson Plan

To support the above lesson plan, a detective log is located on the next page. Copy the log for each new week of observations noting the week number at the top of the page.

Observations

My Information Detective Log

Week # __________

Monday	
Tuesday	
Wednesday	
Thursday	
Friday	

"See what I did!"

The *Ending Stage* of the Research Process

Introduction

Teaching Ideas

Activity Pages

Lesson Plans

Print Support for Lesson Plans

PART III: THE *ENDING STAGE* OF THE RESEARCH PROCESS

Introduction

At this stage of the research process, children will have organized their information for presentation. Research indicates that students at this stage experience increased confidence as they look forward to presenting the results of their research.

The following are teaching ideas and activities for the *ending stage* of the research process. They are products that can be shared with classmates, parents, and school wide.

Teaching Ideas (for the ending stage of research)

1	**Title**: All About Caterpillars and Butterflies: Class Web Site
	Learning Objective(s): Students contribute their information products to the library Web site.
	What to Do: Create a Web site consisting of all that students have learned. Include student work. A nice touch would be to create a blog for parents. This would enable them to read the reflections by LMS and teacher on what has been accomplished at specific intervals in the project. Pages could include Facts About Caterpillars and Butterflies, Different Kinds of Butterflies, What They Eat, and Poems and Riddles About Caterpillars and Butterflies created by individual class members. If you have created a caterpillar habitat, take pictures throughout the life cycle and upload them to the life cycle page. To tie in technology, discuss how technology such as the Web allows people to share information just like your students - even over a great distance.
	Standards Addressed: **Information Power**: Produces and communicates information and ideas in appropriate formats (3.4) **Subject Area**: Language Arts 10.0; Science, (Level 1) 6.0, 6.1; (Level 2) 6.3; Technology 6.4

2	**Title**: Class Picture Dictionary on Caterpillars and Butterflies (K-2)
	Learning Objective(s): 1. Students demonstrate facts and concepts learned through their research. 2. Students can use dictionary skills to organize their topic dictionary. 3. Students work cooperatively to produce a research product in the form of a picture dictionary.
	What to Do: This research product will not only provide an interesting showcase for student knowledge but it will reinforce dictionary skills students have been building and practicing. As a pre-activity, have students recall how a dictionary is used including its organization, presentation of definitions, and so on. Then, brainstorm as many words as possible that students encountered in the course of their research recording them as you go. These could include words related to life cycle (e.g., egg, larva, chrysalis, pupa, butterfly, metamorphosis, etc.), classification, plant life (as food sources), observations made, parts of caterpillars, insects, habitats, and so on. Each student selects (or is assigned) a word for which they will create a picture dictionary page (kindergarten students will require assistance in entering definitions but should have lots of fun with the drawing). Use the "My Picture Dictionary Page" activity provided in the next section as a possible format. When all pages are complete, have students organize the pages alphabetically, create a colorful dictionary cover, and bind. Keep their research product on display in the LMC for next year's class.
	Standards Addressed: **Information Power**: Uses information accurately and creatively (3.0), Organizes information for practical application (3.1); Develops creative products in a variety of formats (5.3) **Subject Area**: Language Arts 1.3; 3.0; 4.0

3	**Title**: Caterpillar and Butterfly (or Insect) Riddles
	Learning Objective(s): Students can relate factual information in a creative format.
	What to Do: You will want to read LMS Jean Maier's lesson plan at the end of Part 3 for a creative research product that primary grade students will love. Once students get a feel for writing riddles, watch out!
	Standards Addressed: See lesson plan.

The following are two teaching ideas that utilize a flannel board as a vehicle for creative storytelling. The first makes use of the storybook and its characters in a very concrete manner that works well with kindergarten students. Number 5 works better as a culmination of research activities.

4	**Title**: The Rest of Squiggly's Story [Note: this is an alternative teaching idea (for #5 below) that makes creating a story even more concrete since students already know the beginning of Squiggly's story]
	Learning Objective(s): 1. Students will use creative media to retell Squiggly's story from the storybook and make up their own middle and ending. 2. Students (at older end of spectrum) understand the basic concept of *point of view* in storytelling. 3. Students incorporate into their stories information gathered in the research process.
	What to Do: The storybook takes students through the beginning phase of research. Have students imagine that the story continues. Brainstorm with students what might happen next? The Curious Kids would explore and collect information that would help Squiggly (middle of story). What would be the ending? They save Squiggly because they find all the information they needed to keep Squiggly alive. As an added touch, they might imagine how the Curious Kids could creatively present what they learned to their friends or family. Encourage students to incorporate facts about caterpillars and butterflies they collected during their research. After brainstorming, break students into pairs or small groups. Assign one student to play the part of Squiggly and the others to play the parts of the Curious Kids and Mac. (Some students can have 2 parts.) For older students, explain point of view and have them tell the story from Squiggly's point of view (i.e., Squiggly as narrator). Encourage applause at the conclusion of the performance.
	Standards Addressed: **Information Power**: Participates effectively in groups to pursue and generate information (9.0); Shares knowledge and information with others (9.1) **Subject Area**: Language Arts 8.0, 8.1

5	**Title**: Our Caterpillar Story (K-1) [Note: Detailed lesson plan for this teaching idea can be found at the end of Part 3 including alternate activities for grades 2-3]
	Learning Objective(s): 1. Students use facts they discovered about their caterpillar/butterfly in the *during stage* of research to tell an original story. 2. Students can identify important story elements.
	What to Do: Create flannel board figures of main characters. Explain or reinforce elements that stories need (e.g., setting, characters, problem, and a solution.) Students work in pairs to create a story that includes at least two facts about their caterpillar/butterfly. The rest can be fiction. At the end of each presentation, ask the presenters' classmates to identify the two facts in the story. Ask them if there is anything that is fictional. Since this is a performance, encourage applause at the conclusion.
	Standards Addressed: See detailed lesson plan at conclusion of Part 3.

6	**Title**: Revisitng the K-W-L Chart from the *Beginning stage* of Research
	Learning Objective(s): Students review what they have learned and the process.
	What to Do: Take out the colorful K-W-L chart created at the beginning of the research project. Revisit what they already knew at the beginning of their project and what they wanted to find out. Then, to review, invite the class to help you fill in the "L" part of the chart with what they "learned" through their research. Since this is the *ending stage* of research and one of our goals is to promote continuing motivation to learn, consider adding an "H" to the chart (K-W-L-H) and discuss with students "how" they could learn more about caterpillars and butterflies or about the insect(s) they researched. Stimulate the desire for continuing their inquiry into the topic on their own.
	Standards Addressed: **Information Power**: Pursues information related to personal interests (4.0) **Subject Area**: Language Arts (Writing) 4.1

The above are just a few ideas for research products that students will enjoy doing while demonstrating new knowledge. There are so many more you could also do. One end product that LMSs and kids enjoy is preparing a newspaper article. Others include creating an informational video in which students interview an expert and recreate their investigation, a brochure for a pretend new butterfly farm, dioramas for young children. Consider integrating what they have learned into an art project that allows them to express themselves creatively.

Activity Pages for Teaching Ideas

On the next page you will find the "My Picture Dictionary" page designed to support teaching idea #2.

For the letter . . .

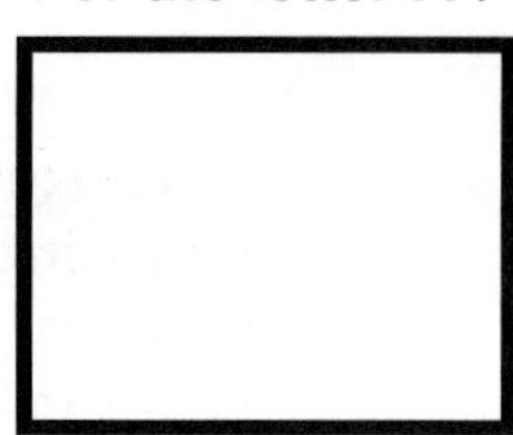

My Picture Dictionary Page
By

Word: ____________________________________

Definition:

____

____

____

Lesson Plans

Two fully described lesson plans are found on the following pages. The first lesson plan was briefly described earlier in teaching idea #5. In addition to K-1 students, the lesson plan includes activities relevant to students in grades 2 and 3.

Lesson Plan Title:
Our Caterpillar Story

Created by: Marie Sciretta and Marilyn Arnone

Stage of Research:	Ending
Grade Levels:	K-3 (procedures indicate grade level activities)
Time Required:	**(K-1):** 1 session for preparation; 1 session for presentation **(2-3):** 2 sessions for preparation; 1 session for presentation
Comments/Notes:	This culminating lesson motivates students by giving them a creative way to showcase their knowledge and achieve recognition from their peers. Students should have been introduced to fact vs. fiction prior to this lesson (see Fact/Fiction activity in Part 1).
Information Literacy Standards:	Uses information accurately and creatively (3.0); Appreciates literature and other creative expressions of information (5.0); Participates effectively in groups to pursue and generate information (9.0)
Related Subject Area(s) and National Content Standards: *(McREL standards)*	Language Arts (Level 1): 1.0, 1.5; 5.0, 5.2; 8.0, 8.4, 8.7 Science (Level 1): 5.0
Learning Goals/Objectives:	1. Students can tell or write an original story using facts about caterpillars and butterflies learned in the *during stage* of research. 2. Students can use both facts and fiction in their story. 3. Students are able to describe story elements.
Required Materials:	Flannel Board (K-1) and character patterns "Our Story Web" activity page (2-3) provided under *Print Support Materials for Lesson Plan* Supplies for book construction (2-3)
Procedures:	NOTE: Since this lesson represents a product of students' research on caterpillars and butterflies, create positive anticipation by building up to it with announcements, colorful posters, and modeling enthusiasm. **Introduction**: Review facts that the class has learned about caterpillars and butterflies. Explain/reinforce story elements (e.g., setting, characters, problem, and solution). Ask students to recall the difference between fact and fiction (see teaching idea #5 in Part 1). Break students into groups. Each group thinks up a name for the main character in their story, the caterpillar.

	(K-1): Use flannel board and figures of story characters (see pattern page). Each group creates a story that includes at least two facts they learned about their caterpillar/butterfly. Other story elements can be fiction. Encourage applause after each group presents their story. Immediately follow-up by asking the rest of the class if they can tell which parts included facts and which parts were fictional. Applaud once more (for both the group and the class as a whole) before moving on to the next group's storytelling presentation. **(2-3):** After reinforcing story elements with the class as a whole, provide each group the "Our Story Web" activity sheet to begin preparing their own story. After each group comes to agreement on their story elements, they can begin writing their story and title. Their stories should include at least four facts as well as fiction. Concentrate first on the text for the story. Then, allow students to illustrate the different pages and the book's cover. The cover should include the title and authors plus a cover illustration. On presentation day, each group reads their story to the whole class with members of the group alternating the reading of each page. Use the follow-up steps as noted in the K-1 procedures.
Learning Assessment(s):	(K-1): Evaluate group stories for facts and fiction. (2-3): Review storybooks for accuracy and creativity. (K-3): Observe whether students are working cooperatively in groups.

Print Support Materials for Lesson Plan

You will find print support materials for the above lesson plan on the next pages. They include the "Our Story Web" activity sheet and "Patterns for Flannel Board and Finger Puppets."

Our Story Web

Patterns for Flannel Board and Finger Puppets

Use this shape to curve and tape to back of patterns when making finger puppets.

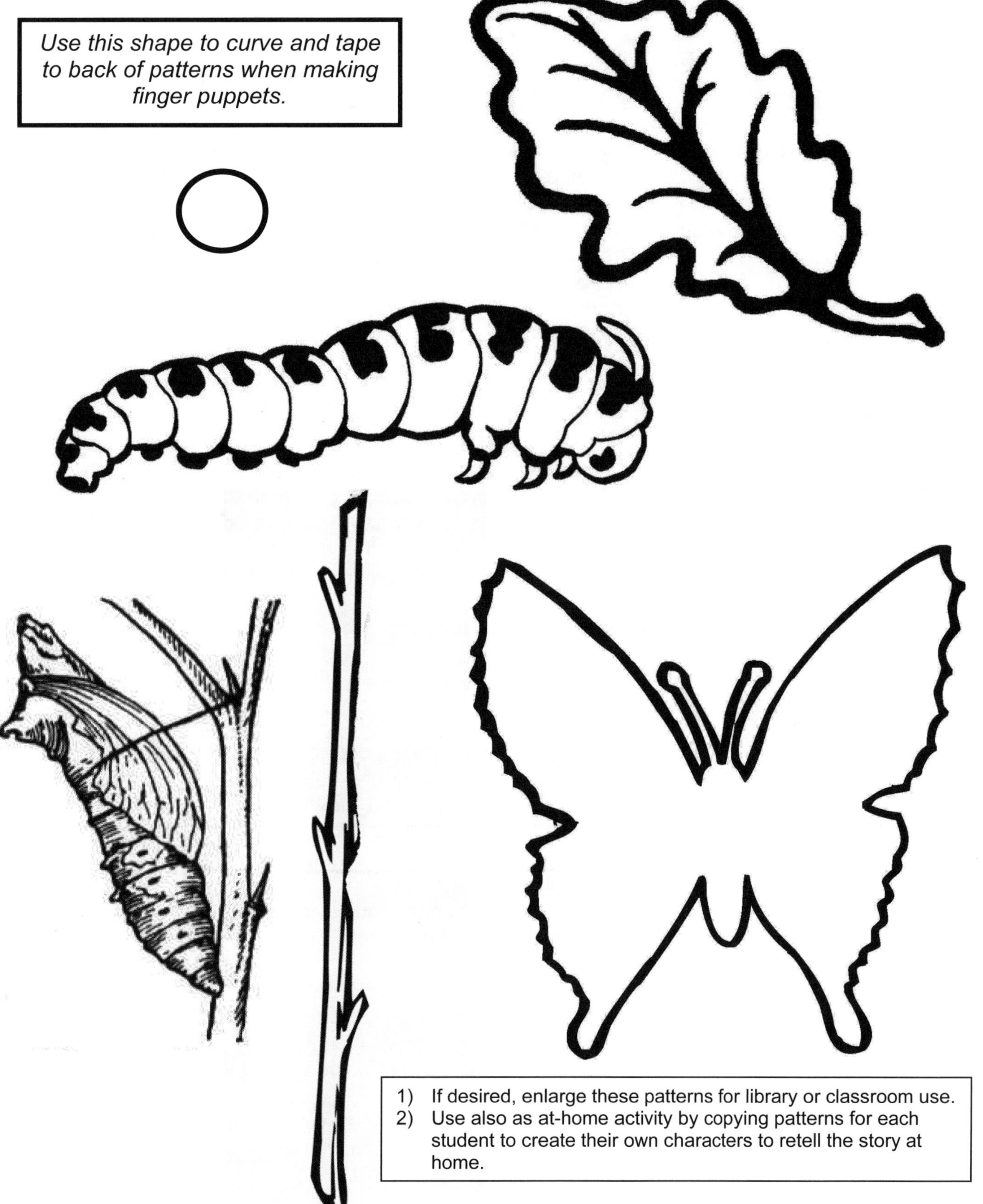

1) If desired, enlarge these patterns for library or classroom use.
2) Use also as at-home activity by copying patterns for each student to create their own characters to retell the story at home.

Lesson Plan Title:
Caterpillar and Butterfly Riddles

Created by: Jean Maier

Stage of Research:	Ending
Grade Levels:	K-2
Time Required:	Several class periods
Comments/Notes:	Children love this lesson. It gives students in primary grades a fun and creative research product that they can share with all.
Information Literacy Standards:	Uses information accurately and creatively (3.0); Produces and communicates information and ideas in appropriate formats (3.4); Shares knowledge and information with others (9.1)
Related Subject Area(s) and National Content Standards: (McREL standards)	Language Arts: (Writing) 1.0
Learning Goals/Objectives:	1. Students will understand the form of a riddle. 2. Students will demonstrate their understanding of the concept of lifecycle of egg-laying animals. 3. Students can apply what they learned in the *during stage* of research to creating their own riddles.
Required Materials:	Books on insects, caterpillars and butterflies Riddle books Paper eggs or chrysalis Glue Lined paper for writing ideas
Procedures:	1. Read students riddles, especially animal riddles. Discuss the form of a riddle. 2. Explain to students that they will be using what they learned about caterpillars and butterflies (or insects) to create their own riddles. 3. Model writing a riddle. 4. Ask students to help you review what they learned in the *during stage* of research. Encourage active participation. 5. From what students generated in the review of research, write ideas on the board or flipchart that students can use to create their riddles (e.g., riddles about what it eats, where it lives, what it looks like, lifecycle, etc.) 6. Students must use facts to write their riddles. They can use any of the books from their research to help them get ideas.

	7. As a final product, glue riddles to the lower half of a paper egg or chrysalis. The answer is written near the top and a half egg is stapled over the answer that can be lifted to reveal the answer. 8. Share and laugh.
Learning Assessment(s):	Are students able to use the facts found in nonfiction books to create an original riddle?

Older children may also enjoy rhyming riddles. Younger children will need much simpler forms for their riddles and assistance in writing them down. For example, an easier form for K-1 students would be:

I begin with the letter ____.

FACT 1

FACT 2

What am I?

Final Thoughts

We hope that this guide has inspired your own imaginative ideas for using the storybook approach of *The Curious Kids and the Squiggly Question* to introduce your Curious Kids to information literacy skills essential to the research process.

References

AASL and AECT, *Information Power: Building Partnerships for Learning* (Chicago: American Library Association, 1998).

Arnone, Marilyn, *The Strangest Dinosaur That Never Was: Educator's Guide*, (Westport, CT: Libraries Unlimited, 2003).

Kuhlthau, Carol, "Inside the Search Process: Seeking from the User's Perspective," *Journal of the American Society of Information Science* 42, no. 5 (1991): 361-371.

Small, Ruth V. and Arnone, Marilyn P., *Turning Kids on to Research: The Power of Motivation* (Westport, CT: Libraries Unlimited, 2000).

Stripling, Barbara K. "Inquiry-Based Learning," in *Curriculum Connections Through the Library: Principles and Practice*, ed. Barbara K. Stripling and Sandra Hughes-Hassell. (Westport, CT: Libraries Unlimited, 2003).